Since God Loves You and You Know It...
SING OUT LOUD!

Fun and Instructional Songs about Church Time Basics, God's Love and Bible Stories for Catholic Children

Original Lyrics set to Traditional Tunes by Christina Romas Connant
Illustrated by Kristen Bannister

Copyright ©2017 Christina Romas Connant

All rights reserved. Thank you for buying an authorized edition of this book and for complying with copyright law by not reproducing, storing in a retrieval system, or transmitting in any form or by any means -- electronic, mechanical, photocopy, recording, scanning, or other -- except for brief quotations in critical reviews or articles, without the prior written permission of the publisher.

Published by Christina Connant
Contact the Publisher at www.SinceGodLovesYou.com

ISBN: 978-0-9860992-2-9 (paperback)
ISBN: 978-0-9860992-3-6 (ebook)

Dedication

I extend a special Thank You to all the children who inspired me to create these songs and to their parents who encouraged me to share these songs with others. My goal is to fill your hearts and souls with God's love and His lessons in a way that captures your attention. I am especially thankful for the support and dedication of my husband, Charles, and our own little angels, Elizabeth and Corinne.

And sincere appreciation to the clergy who provided spiritual guidance and advice:

- The Reverend Father Peter Delvizis (Greek Orthodox)
- The Reverend Krista Dias (Episcopal)
- The Reverend Jennifer Testa Hrynyk (Protestant)
- Anthanasios Minetos, Pastoral Assistant (Greek Orthodox)
- The Very Reverend Father Robert Stephanopoulos (Greek Orthodox)
- Deacon Michael Wojcik (Catholic)

Table of Contents

Welcome 6
Welcome Educators and Parents 7
Hello, Hello 8

Church Time Basics 10
Quietly 11
Three Persons of God -- The Trinity 12
Sign of the Cross 13
This Great God 14
Five Little Kids 16
Listening so Joyfully 18
Sacraments 20
I'm a Sweet Little Catholic Child 22
The Kids Go Marching to the Church 24
The Offering Basket 25

God Loves Us 26
God Loves Everyone 27
Since God Loves You and You Know It 28
Skinamarinky Dinky Dink 29
God Gave Us Someone Who Loves 30

Bible Stories 32
Listen to the Bible 33

Bible Stories -- Old Testament 34
Adam and Eve 35
Noah 36
Old Man Noah 37
Jacob's Ladder 38
Joseph was a Dreamer 39
Moses 40
Gideon's Trumpet 41
Samuel and Eli 42
David Beat Goliath 43
Elijah and the Ravens 44
Daniel in the Lion's Den 45
Jonah and the Whale 46

Bible Stories -- New Testament 48
Mary Had a Little Lamb 49
John the Baptist 50
Wedding of Cana 51
Jesus' Miracles 52
Good Samaritan 53
Palm Sunday and Last Supper 54

Lent and Easter/Pascha 56
Easter's Coming 57
Easter is a Special Time 58
Christos Anesti is What We Say 59
This is Pentecost 60

Helpful Hints 62

Sample Circle Time Lessons 63

About the Author 64

How It Started 65

WELCOME

Welcome Educators and Parents!

Get ready to enlighten your children about God's love for us all in a delightful and interactive way. This book approaches teaching the simplest Bible Stories and Church Time Basics by use of well known and traditional melodies -- but with a twist. The lyrics of each song have original adaptations and are intended to teach church fundamentals with an appealing and understandable approach. By using familiar tunes, children are able to learn about the teachings and traditions of our faith -- while allowing them to recognize things that we see and do in church. Suggestions for your own Circle Time lessons are at the back of this book.

Listen to the songs at www.SinceGodLovesYou.com by entering the password: "Sunny Sings".

Look for the lamb, Sunny, to give you and your little ones some extra guidance and instruction.

Since God Loves You and You Know It...
SING OUT LOUD!

This edition has some songs specific for Catholic Children.
Our friends of other traditions can see the other editions:

- For Orthodox Christian Children
- For Christian Children

Hello, Hello

Hello, hello we're glad you're here today
To church, to church to learn about our faith

Let's say hello to _____ we're glad you came today
Jesus loves the little children and He's glad you're here today

(Repeat with each child's name)

Songs can be heard on www.SinceGodLovesYou.com, enter the password: "Sunny Sings".

WELCOME

CHURCH TIME BASICS

There are many things that we see and do in church -- some things vary by religious denomination others vary by individual parish. Find the songs that fit your customs and beliefs to share with your children.

Quietly

(to the tune of "I'm Bringing Home a Baby Bumblebee", traditional nursery rhyme)

When we go to church, we need to sit quietly and respectfully and not disturb the other people, so we can all listen to the service.

I'm walking into church so quietly
Won't my mommy be so proud of me
'Cause I'm walking into church so quietly
Shh, shh, shh, shh, shh (put finger to lips in "shush" gesture)

I'm listening to the priest so silently
Won't my mommy be so proud of me
'Cause I'm listening to the priest so silently
Shh, shh, shh, shh, shh (put finger to lips in "shush" gesture)

I'm sitting in the church respectfully
Won't my mommy be so proud of me
'Cause I'm sitting in the church respectfully
Shh, shh, shh, shh, shh (put finger to lips in "shush" gesture)

Additional optional verses:

- I'm praying in the church so peacefully...
- I'm thanking God in church so lovingly...
- I'm holding my candle so carefully...

CHURCH TIME BASICS

Three Persons of God -- The Trinity

(to the tune of "Three Blind Mice", traditional nursery rhyme)

Three Persons of God, Three Persons of God (Hold up three fingers)
They are One, They are One (Hold up one finger)
Father, Son and Spirit Holy
All are God equally
Also called the Trinity
Three Persons of God, They are One (Hold up three fingers)

Two Natures of Christ, Two Natures of Christ (Hold up two fingers)
At the same time, At the same time
Christ the Man that walked on ground
Christ the God who's all around
Our belief is quite profound
Two Natures of Christ, At the same time (Hold up two fingers)

The three fingers the Orthodox hold together represent the Trinity -- the Father, the Son and the Holy Spirit. The two fingers then remain down to represent the Two Natures of Christ -- Divine and Human.

Sign of the Cross
(to the tune of "Are You Sleeping?", traditional nursery rhyme)

Christians often "cross themselves" as a sign of their faith -- to do this we take our right hand and move it across our body, starting at our forehead, our tummy (or heart), then from one shoulder to the opposite shoulder. Catholics touch their left shoulder first.

This song demonstrates how to do this.

Raise your right hand, raise your right hand
    (raise up your right hand, and your child's right hand)
Just like this, just like this
    (hold hand open with palm facing body)
Place it on your forehead
    (guide your child's hand to their forehead)
Then down to your tummy
    (guide your child's hand to their tummy)
Shoulder, shoulder
    (guide your child's hand to their left shoulder
    then to right shoulder)
We made our cross
    (guide your childs hands together; fingers up toward
    Heaven, in prayer gesture)

CHURCH TIME BASICS

This Great God

(to the tune of "This Old Man", traditional nursery rhyme)

This Great God, He made one (hold up one finger)
He gave us Jesus His only Son
With the Light of the World and the Sign of the Cross
　　(raise both hands toward Heaven then make Cross with hands)
We all know that God is Boss

This Great God, He made two (hold up two fingers)
He made the animals in the zoo
With the Light of the World and the Sign of the Cross
　　(raise both hands toward Heaven then make Cross with hands)
We all know that God is Boss

This Great God, He made three (hold up three fingers)
He loves you and He loves me
With the Light of the World and the Sign of the Cross
　　(raise both hands toward Heaven then make Cross with hands)
We all know that God is Boss

This Great God, He made four (hold up four fingers)
He rules the earth and so much more
With the Light of the World and the Sign of the Cross
    (raise both hands toward Heaven then make Cross with hands)
We all know that God is Boss

This Great God, He made five (hold up five fingers)
He makes us happy we're alive
With the Light of the World and the Sign of the Cross
    (raise both hands toward Heaven then make Cross with hands)
We all know that God is Boss

God is so Great -- He made everyone and everything in the world and loves all His creations.

Five Little Kids

(to the tune of "Five Little Ducks", nursery rhyme)

Five little kids in church today
They wanted to come here on Sunday
The first one bent down on one knee
Then sat down respectfully

Five little kids in church today
They wanted to come here on Sunday
The second one went into the line
For the Communion bread and wine

Five little kids in church today
They wanted to come here on Sunday
The third one didn't make a peep
And sat right in his very own seat

Five little kids in church today
They wanted to come here on Sunday
The fourth one didn't run or hide
But stood right next to their parent's side

Five little kids in church today
They wanted to come here on Sunday
The fifth one prayed about her day
And was dismissed in a peaceful way

Listening so Joyfully
(to the tune of "Ode to Joy")

Music is an important part of many church services. There are different styles of music, and all the music helps the people remember the teachings and feel special connections too.

Children sitting in the church pew
Listening so joyfully
Hear the choir singing praises
Hear the cantor chanting hymns
"Lord have mercy, Alleluia
Kyrie Eleison"
We can hear angelic voices
"Praise the Lord and Amen"

A "pew" is another word for a church seat.

18 CHURCH TIME BASICS

Sacraments

(to the tune of "She'll Be Coming 'Round the Mountain", traditional folk song)

Holy Sacraments are important parts of a Christian's life. The seven Sacraments are: Baptism, Holy Communion, Confirmation (Chrismation), Confession (Reconciliation), Matrimony (Marriage), Anointing the Sick or Unction and Ordination (Holy Orders).

There are seven Sacraments for Christians
There are seven Sacraments for Christians
There are seven Sacraments, there are seven Sacraments,
 there are seven Sacraments for Christians

We're born into our life of Christ with Baptism
We're born into our life of Christ with Baptism
We're born into our life of Christ, we are born into our life of Christ,
 we're born into our life of Christ with Baptism

We become one with Jesus Christ through Communion
We become one with Jesus Christ through Communion
We become one with Jesus Christ, we become one with Jesus Christ,
 we become one with Jesus Christ through Communion

To shorten the song, you may choose to sing the first verse and the verse that relates to the Sacrament you are teaching that day.

We strengthen our Christian faith through Chrismation
We strengthen our Christian faith through Chrismation
We strengthen our Christian faith through,
    we strengthen our Christian faith through,
        we strengthen our Christian faith through Chrismation

We're forgiven for our sins through Confession
We're forgiven for our sins through Confession
We're forgiven for our sins, we're forgiven for our sins,
    we're forgiven for our sins through Confession

When our Moms and Dads got married, that's Marriage
When our Moms and Dads got married, that's Marriage
When our Moms and Dads got married, when our Moms and Dads got married,
    when our Moms and Dads got married that's Marriage

Christ heals our souls and bodies through Anointing
Christ heals our souls and bodies through Anointing
Christ heals our souls and bodies, Christ heals our souls and bodies,
    Christ heals our souls and bodies through Anointing

Chosen men serve the Lord through Ordination
Chosen men serve the Lord through Ordination
Chosen men serve the Lord, chosen men serve the Lord,
    chosen men serve the Lord through Ordination

I'm a Sweet Little Catholic Child

(to the tune of "I Have a Little Nut Tree", traditional nursery rhyme)

I'm a sweet little Catholic child
Here is my heart and here is my smile
(place hand on heart then hands on cheeks of smiling face)
My parents bring me to the church on Sunday
That is where I learn about God and pray!
    (fold hands together in prayer)

The Kids Go to Marching to the Church

(to the tune of "The Ants Go Marching", traditional folk song)

The kids go marching to the church to pray, to pray
The kids go marching to the church to pray, to pray
Dip their hand into the water font
Make their cross and think of God
And the kids go marching to the church to pray, to pray

The kids go quietly to the church to pray, to pray
The kids go quietly to the church to pray, to pray
They sit and listen attentively
To the priest during the Liturgy
And the kids sit in church so quietly, so quietly

The kids line up for Communion to receive, receive
The kids line up for Communion to receive, receive
They open their hands to make the Throne
Open their hearts and receive the Host
When they receive the Body and Blood of Christ

Eucharist is another word for Communion.

The Offering Basket
(to the tune of "A Tisket A Tasket" traditional nursery rhyme)

The basket, the basket
I see a wicker basket
I get some money from my purse
And make an offering to the church

The offering, the offering
Why do I give an offering?
It helps us do the work of God
And a "thank you" for my blessings

Sometimes a tray, or plate is used for the offering, but it is still for the good works of the church.

CHURCH TIME BASICS

GOD LOVES US

God loves all people --
that means me and you and everyone!

God Loves Everyone

(to the tune of "Mary Had a Little Lamb", traditional nursery rhyme)

God loves me and God loves you (point to yourself, then point to others)
God loves us, God loves us (open arms to show inclusion of all)
God loves me and God loves you (point to yourself, then point to others)
God loves everyone! (open arms to show inclusion of all)

Since God Loves You and You Know It

(to the tune of "If You're Happy and You Know It", traditional folk song)

Since God loves you and you know it, Clap your hands
Since God loves you and you know it, Clap your hands
Since God loves you and you know it and you really want to show it
Since God loves you and you know it, Clap your hands

Since God loves you and you know it, Stomp your feet
Since God loves you and you know it, Stomp your feet
Since God loves you and you know it and you really want to show it
Since God loves you and you know it, Stomp your feet

Since God loves you and you know it, Blow a kiss
Since God loves you and you know it, Blow a kiss
Since God loves you and you know it and you really want to show it
Since God loves you and you know it, Blow a kiss

Since God loves you and you know it, Shout Amen
Since God loves you and you know it, Shout Amen
Since God loves you and you know it and you really want to show it
Since God loves you and you know it, Shout Amen

We can show our love in many joyous ways -- how else can you show God's love?

Skinamarinky Dinky Dink

Skinamarinky Dinky Dink
Skinamarinky Do
God loves you
He loves you in the morning,
And in the afternoon
He loves you in the evening
And underneath the moon
Skinamarinky Dinky Dink
Skinamarinky Do
God loves you!

God loves us all the time -- both day and night.

GOD LOVES US

God Gave Us Someone Who Loves

(to the tune of "BINGO", traditional nursery rhyme)

God loves each of us, just as Mommy and Daddy love us.

God gave us someone who loves
And Mommy is her name-o
M-O-M-M-Y, M-O-M-M-Y, M-O-M-M-Y
And Mommy is her name-o

God gave us someone who loves
And Daddy is his name-o
D-A-D-D-Y, D-A-D-D-Y, D-A-D-D-Y
And Daddy is his name-o

God gave us someone who loves
And Jesus is His name-o
J-E-S-U-S, J-E-S-U-S, J-E-S-U-S
And Jesus is His name-o

God gave us many people who love us --
who else can you think of?

GOD LOVES US

BIBLE STORIES

These songs are best accompanied by your favorite children's Bible on hand and using it to reinforce the lessons in stories.

Listen to the Bible

(to the tune of "Hush Little Baby", traditional lullaby)

Hush little children,
Don't say a word
Listen to the Bible
And hear God's Word

Stories written
A long time ago
In two parts
An Old and a New

People with names like
Moses and Noah
Adam and Eve and
Also Jonah

Four Gospels tell us
About Jesus Christ
Lots of stories
About His life

Hush little children
Don't say a word
Listen to the Bible
And hear God's Word

BIBLE STORIES

BIBLE STORIES
OLD TESTAMENT

The Old Testament is the older part of the Bible, about things that happened before Jesus was born. These are the stories He studied.

Adam and Eve

(to the tune of "Camptown Races", traditional folk song)

Don't eat from the apple tree
No no, no no
Don't eat from the apple tree
God warned Adam and Eve
God warned Adam and Eve
Don't eat from the tree
Don't eat from the apple tree
Or you'll have to leave

Come eat from the apple tree
Yoo-hoo, yoo-hoo
Come eat from the apple tree
The snake said to Adam and Eve
The snake said to Adam and Eve
Come eat from the tree
They ate from the apple tree
And God told them to leave

Genesis 2-3

OLD TESTAMENT

Noah

(to the tune of "Rain Rain Go Away", traditional nursery rhyme)

Rain, rain for 40 days
Noah built a boat to stay
His family kept the faith and prayed
The white dove brought a brand new day

Genesis 6-9

Old Man Noah

(to the tune of "Old MacDonald", traditional nursery rhyme)

Old man Noah had an arc --
    E-I-E-I-O
And on that arc he has TWO (animal of your choice, ex. duck) --
    E-I-E-I-O
With a – (ex. quack, quack) here and a – (ex. quack, quack) there
Here a – (ex. quack), there a – (ex. quack)
Everywhere a – (ex. quack, quack)
Old man Noah had an arc --
    E-I-E-I-O

(Repeat with other animals.)

Genesis 6-9

OLD TESTAMENT

Jacob's Ladder

(to the tune of "Ring Around the Rosie", traditional nursery rhyme)

On a rock Jacob was sleeping
'Bout a ladder he was dreaming
Angels, angels going up and down

God said, "I'll be good to you"
Jacob said, "I'll follow you"
Angels, angels going up and down

Genesis 28

OLD TESTAMENT

Joseph was a Dreamer

(to the tune of "Lavendar Blue", traditional nursery rhyme)

Lavender blue -- diddle diddle,
    orange and pink
Joseph's new coat -- diddle diddle
From his dad was a gift

His dad liked him best -- diddle diddle,
    His brothers got mad
They didn't like him -- diddle diddle
And they treated him bad

Joseph had dreams -- diddle diddle,
    And they came true
He told the King -- diddle diddle
What he should do

He told the King -- diddle diddle,
    You must save the grain
Cause for seven years -- diddle diddle
There won't be much rain

They all had food -- diddle diddle,
    Thanks to Joseph's cue
The people were saved -- diddle diddle
And his brothers were too

Genesis 38-47

OLD TESTAMENT

Moses

(to the tune of "Here We Go Round the Mulberry Bush", traditional folk song)

Moses saw a burning bush,
      burning bush, burning bush
Moses saw a burning bush
And God spoke to him

Take your people from Egypt now,
      Egypt now, Egypt now
Take your people from Egypt now
And God will keep them safe

God gave Moses Ten Rules of Life,
      Rules of Life, Rules of Life
God gave Moses Ten Rules of Life
Called the Commandments

Exodus 3-20

OLD TESTAMENT

Gideon's Trumpet

(to the tune of "Skip to My Lou", traditional folk song)

Gideon's trumpet goes -- toot-toot-toot
Gideon's jars broke -- boom, boom, boom
Gideon's torches burned -- look, look, look
"We're the sword of the Lord," they shouted

Confused the enemy -- who, who, who
Attacked each other -- shoot, shoot, shoot
His tiny army -- won, won, won
Beat them without fighting!

Judges 6-8

OLD TESTAMENT

Samuel and Eli

(to the tune of "Baa Baa Black Sheep", traditional folk song)

"Samuel, Samuel," a voice was in his dream
"Eli, Eli -- did you call my name?"
"It wasn't me, just go back to sleep"
Then he learned it was God who speaks
"Samuel, Samuel -- Listen, it's the Lord"
Samuel always did what he was told

1 Samuel 1-4

David Beat Goliath

(to the tune of "London Bridges", traditional nursery rhyme)

David was a shepherd boy, shepherd boy, shepherd boy
David was a shepherd boy -- with God's blessings

Goliath was looking for a fight, for a fight, for a fight
Goliath was looking for a fight -- against the army

David's stone knocked him down, knocked him down, knocked him down
David's stone knocked him down -- David beat Goliath!

1 Samuel 17

Elijah and the Ravens

(to the tune of "Sing a Song of Sixpence", traditional nursery rhyme)

There was no rain for many years
The rivers were all dry
Elijah saw some blackbirds flying in the sky
Those ravens brought him meat -- and a piece of bread
Everyday God sent them, so he would be fed

He also needed water, so that he could drink
The Lord showed Elijah a little hidden creek
Then one day that dried up -- a woman he would seek
Every day she baked them bread so they both could eat

1 Kings 16-17

Daniel in the Lion's Den

(to the tune of "Do you know the Muffin Man?", traditional nursery rhyme)

The king put Daniel in the lion's den, the lion's den, the lion's den
The king put Daniel in the lion's den
Because he prayed to God

An angel came to keep Daniel safe, Daniel safe, Daniel safe
An angel came to keep Daniel safe
Because he prayed to God

Daniel 6

OLD TESTAMENT

Jonah and the Whale

(to the tune of "Take Me out to the Ball Game", original music, 1908)

God asked Jonah to help him
Tell the bad people to stop
He ran away onto a boat instead
When the storm came, "Throw me out," he said

The storm suddenly calmed down
And inside a whale he prayed
After one, two, three days he's out
Of the whale all saved

Jonah 1-2

BIBLE STORIES
NEW TESTAMENT

The New Testament is the newer part of the Bible, about Jesus and things that happened after Jesus was born.

Mary Had a Little Lamb

(to the tune of "Mary Had a Little Lamb", traditional nursery rhyme)

Mary had a little lamb,
Little lamb, little lamb
Mary had a little lamb
And JESUS was his name

He made the world a brighter place,
Brighter place, brighter place
He made the world a brighter place
His life's a gift for us

Matthew 1, Luke 2

"Behold, the Lamb of God who takes away the sin of the world!" – John 1:29

NEW TESTAMENT

John the Baptist -- Epiphany

(to the tune of "Jack and Jill", traditional nursery rhyme)

The Baptist John
With camel coat on
Was at the Jordan River
The Spirit Above
Appeared as a Dove
When Jesus came out of the water

"This is my Son
The Chosen One"
Came a voice from heaven
"I am the Light
That brings you life"
Jesus said to His brethren

Matthew 3, John 1-8

"Brethern" are "brothers" or friends of Jesus.

Wedding of Cana

(to the tune of "Farmer in the Dell", traditional nursery rhyme)

In Cana of Galilee
There was a big party
Jesus' first great miracle
Was in Cana of Galilee

At the big wedding
The wine was all empty
Jesus' first great miracle
Was at the big wedding

He turned water into wine
It tasted really fine
Jesus' first great miracle
When water turned to wine

John 2

"Miracles" are when something really special happens that normal people cannot do, but God or Jesus can make happen.

NEW TESTAMENT

Jesus' Miracles

(to the tune of "Wheels on the Bus", anonymous folk song)

Jesus made the sick person get better,
Get better, get better
Jesus made the sick person get better
'Twas a miracle

Jesus made the blind man see, see, see
See, see, see -- see, see, see
Jesus made the blind man see, see, see
'Twas a miracle

Jesus turned the bread into many loaves
Many loaves, many loaves
Jesus turned the bread into many loaves
'Twas a miracle

Jesus helped the fishermen catch the fish
Catch the fish, catch the fish
Jesus helped the fishermen catch the fish
'Twas a miracle

Luke 17,
John 9, Mark 10,
Matthew 14,
Luke 5

Good Samaritan (The Golden Rule)

(to the tune of "Itsy Bitsy Spider", traditional nursery rhyme)

There once was a man who was walking down the street
Along came a thief who knocked him off his feet
All the people passing by left him there in pain
'But the Good Samaritan who helped him up again

Jesus told this story as a message to us all
We need to help people, 'specially when they fall
"Be a good neighbor and help your friends and foe"
This is the lesson He wants us all to know.

Luke 10

The Golden Rule says "Be good to others and treat them like you want them to treat you."

NEW TESTAMENT

Palm Sunday and Last Supper

(to the tune of "Yankee Doodle", traditional folk song)

Jesus Christ went to town
Riding on a donkey
Everyone called Him their King
And waved leaves from a palm tree

Jesus met with His 12 friends
For His Last Supper
He broke the bread and blessed the wine
For all to remember

Mark 11-14

LENT and EASTER / PASCHA

Easter's Coming
(to the tune of "Spring is Coming")

On the third Sunday of Orthodox Lent (the Adoration of the Cross), a daffodil usually is given out to everyone. This is a symbol of the Resurrection, or new life, since the daffodil is one of the first flowers to bloom in the spring. It signifies the approach of Easter/Pascha*.

Spring is coming, spring is coming
How do you think I know?
I saw a yellow daffodil
I know it must be so!

Easter's coming, Easter's coming
How do you think I know?
I got a yellow daffodil
I know it must be so!

*The word "Easter" can be replaced by "Pascha" based on your preference.

Easter is a Special Time

(to the tune of "Pop Goes the Weasel", traditional nursery rhyme)

Easter is a special time
We prepare by fasting
Jesus died to save our souls
For life everlasting!

We prepare for 40 days
Of Lent to cleanse our spirit
We give up foods like meat and cheese
And try to act with kindness

Easter is a special time
A time for new beginnings
Jesus died to help us all
Go UP into heaven!

Lent is a time when we try to focus on God. We simplify our lives by giving up certain foods, or other material goods. We try to live God's love by helping others and acting kindly.

Christos Anesti is What We Say

(to the tune of "He's Got the Whole World in His Hands")

Christos Anesti is Greek for "Christ is Risen", a common greeting among Orthodox Christians during Easter and the 40 days that follow. Alithos Anetsi is Greek for "Truly He is Risen", the usual response.

Christos Anesti is what we say
Christos Anesti is what we say
Christos Anesti is what we say
Christ rose on Easter Day

Alithos Anesti is our reply
Alithos Anesti is our reply
Alithos Anesti is our reply
Christ rose up to the sky

LENT and EASTER/PASCHA

This is Pentecost

(to the tune of "For He's a Jolly Good Fellow")

It's 50 days after Easter
It's 50 days after Easter
It's 50 days after Easter
This is Pentecost

It's the Church's birthday
It's the Church's birthday
It's the Church's birthday
This is Pentecost

Let's all spread the Good News
Let's all spread the Good News
Let's all spread the Good News
About Christ our Lord

Helpful Hints

This is more than just a book, it is a program geared towards young children (ages 1-5) to become familiar with basic church teachings and behavior. It uses simple Bible stories set to familiar lay tunes. Children tend to be more attentive to simple songs and retain lessons when they hear things in nursery rhyme style songs. All the tunes chosen are traditional and familiar ones, that most everyone already knows. The words have all been adapted to effectively teach our children God's message: That God loves us all.

- Keep it fun!

- Repetition is key -- daily, weekly -- as often as you like -- children love familiarity, which helps them master their world.

- Don't worry if the children don't sit and listen like perfect angels -- even if they do not sit still and pay full attention, they are probably still listening. It is always surprising to find out what they are hearing!

- Keep your expectations realistic for the attention span of young children -- a circle time of between 15-30 minutes is recommended, but can be shorter or longer based on your group of children on a given day.

Songs can be heard on www.SinceGodLovesYou.com with the password: "Sunny Sings"

Sample Circle Time Lessons

Usually choose 8-12 songs and read a short Bible Story in the middle.

→ Welcome
- Sign of the Cross
- Three Persons of God
- Five Little Kids
- I'm a Sweet Little Catholic Child
- Hush Little Children

→ Read a Children's Bible Story
→ Sing Corresponding song to Bible Story
- God Loves Us
- Since God Loves You and You Know It
- Quietly

→ Welcome
- Quietly
- Sacraments
- This Great God
- Listening so Joyfully
- Hush Little Children

→ Read a Children's Bible Story)
→ Sing Corresponding song to Bible Story
- God Gave Us Someone Who Loves
- Skinamarinky Dinky Dink
- Since God Loves You and You Know It

→ Welcome
- Sign of the Cross
- Mary Had a Little Lamb
- This Great God
- The Offering Basket
- Hush Little Children

→ Read a Children's Bible Story
→ Sing Corresponding song to Bible Story
- Good Samaritan
- God Loves Us
- Since God Loves You and You Know It

→ Welcome
- Sign of the Cross
- The Kids Go Marching to the Church
- The Offering Basket
- Hush Little Children

→ Read a Children's Bible Story
- Easter's Coming
- Easter is a Special Time
- Christos Anesti is What We Say
- Since God Loves You and You Know It
- Quietly

About the Author

Christina Romas Connant has dedicated her life to the service of others. From an early age, the church has played a very powerful role in her development. Her love for wholesome values, learning, and the sharing of ideas have shaped her into a dedicated and influential Sunday School teacher. For well over ten years, her classes strive to make church teachings accessible and understandable to children of all ages, including the very young. She accomplishes this through various methods, including original instructional songs. Christina gives countless hours of her time and expertise to various non-profit organizations, ranging from the Metropolitan Museum of Art, The Junior League, Girl Scouts and in the local schools. She lives in New Jersey with her wonderful husband and two inspiring daughters.

This is her first book, with ideas for more in the works!
Go to www.SinceGodLovesYou.com or follow her on Facebook to see what else Christina is working on, or let her know what you'd like to see next!

About the Illustrator

Kristen Bannister is a graphic designer and creator of Amelia, an adorable penguin. Check out www.ameliasgreetings.com to see her collection of greeting cards and stationery.

How It Started

Before Christina had children of her own, she taught Sunday School to elementary school aged children. Once she became a mother, she moved to the Nursery class, which was geared for 0-3 year old children. She wanted to make the class more than just a "cry room", but actually provide some religious education. She tried to read from a children's Bible, and in an attempt to have the children sit and listen, she provided a snack. But once the animal crackers ran out, they did not pay much attention to the story.

As a mother of her own young children, she noticed that if she sang almost anything, her children calmed down and listened. She saw that most children loved the soothing and familiar tunes of Nursery Rhymes. Those melodies became the base for all the lyrics. The words and songs in this book are the outcome of her time with the children each and every Sunday. There are so many basic concepts she wanted to teach, and before she knew it -- over 40 songs were written!

Parents loved it as much as the kids -- and encouraged Christina to publish these songs to share with all of you!

www.ingramcontent.com/pod-product-compliance
Lightning Source LLC
Chambersburg PA
CBHW041430090426
42744CB00002B/16